MARIAH CAREY
EMOTIONS

ISBN 0-7935-1210-7

Hal Leonard Publishing Corporation
7777 West Bluemound Road P.O. Box 13819 Milwaukee, WI 53213

Copyright © 1992 by HAL LEONARD PUBLISHING CORPORATION
International Copyright Secured   All Rights Reserved

For all works contained herein:
Unauthorized copying, arranging, adapting, recording or public performance is an infringement of copyright.
Infringers are liable under the law.

EMOTIONS
MARIAH CAREY

14   AND YOU DON'T REMEMBER

18   CAN'T LET GO

8   EMOTIONS

34   IF IT'S OVER

24   MAKE IT HAPPEN

50   SO BLESSED

70   TILL THE END OF TIME

56   TO BE AROUND YOU

64   THE WIND

41   YOU'RE SO COLD

EMOTIONS

Lyrics by MARIAH CAREY
Music by MARIAH CAREY, DAVID COLE and ROBERT CLIVILLES

MAKE IT HAPPEN

Lyrics by MARIAH CAREY
Music by MARIAH CAREY, DAVID COLE and ROBERT CLIVILLES

Copyright © 1991 Sony Songs Inc., Mariah Carey Songs, Virgin Music, Inc. and Cole/Clivilles Music
All Rights on behalf of Sony Songs Inc. and Mariah Carey Songs administered by Sony Music Publishing
All Rights for Cole/Clivilles Music Controlled and Administered by Virgin Music, Inc. (ASCAP)
International Copyright Secured   All Rights Reserved

YOU'RE SO COLD

Lyrics by MARIAH CAREY
Music by MARIAH CAREY and DAVID COLE

SO BLESSED

Lyrics by MARIAH CAREY
Music by MARIAH CAREY and WALTER AFANASIEFF

Copyright © 1991 Sony Songs Inc., Mariah Carey Songs, WB Music Corp. and Wallyworld
All Right on behalf of Sony Songs Inc. and Mariah Carey Songs administered by Sony Music Publishing
All rights on behalf of Wallyworld administered by WB Music Corp.
International Copyright Secured   All Rights Reserved

THE WIND

New Lyrics by MARIAH CAREY
Music by RUSSELL FREEMAN

Copyright © 1991 Encore Music
International Copyright Secured   All Rights Reserved

TILL THE END OF TIME

Lyrics by MARIAH CAREY
Music by MARIAH CAREY and WALTER AFANASIEFF

(Ooh, love you till the end of time.)

(Ooh, baby I would love you till the end of time.)

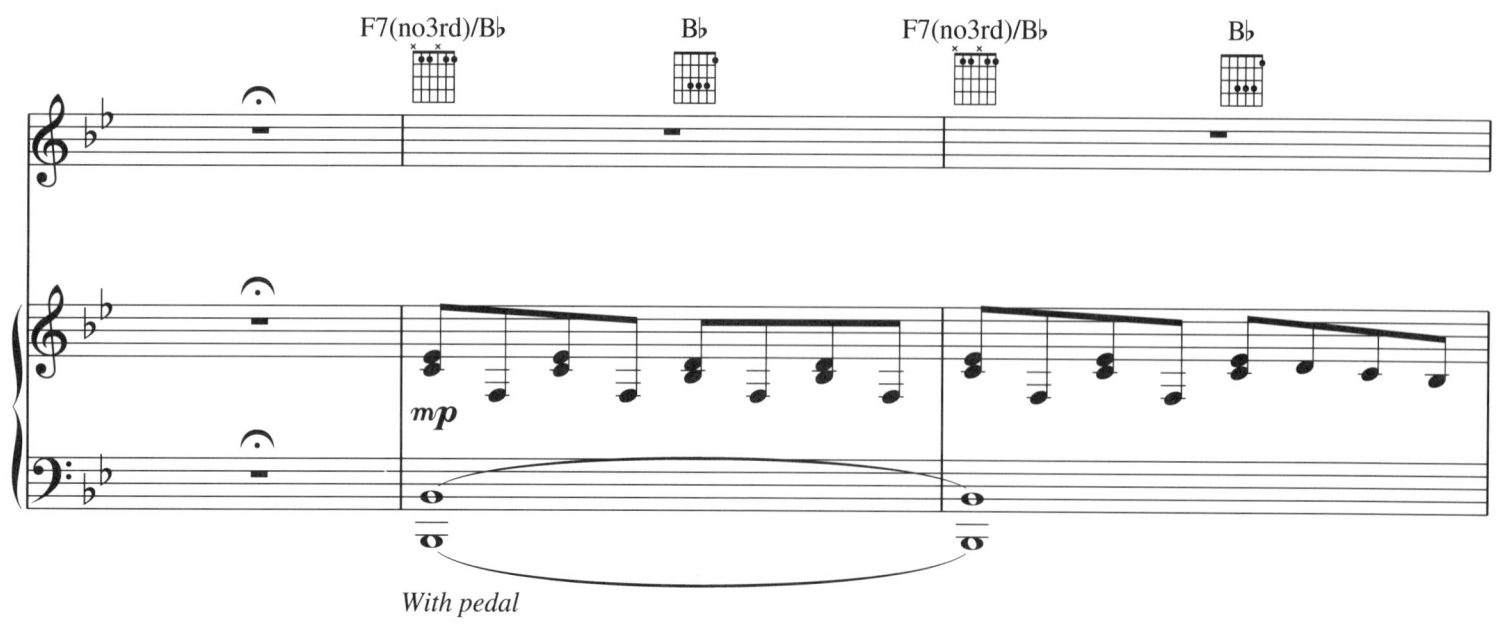

Copyright © 1991 Sony Songs Inc., Mariah Carey Songs, WB Music Corp. and Wallyworld
All Right on behalf of Sony Songs Inc. and Mariah Carey Songs administered by Sony Music Publishing
All rights on behalf of Wallyworld administered by WB Music Corp.
International Copyright Secured   All Rights Reserved

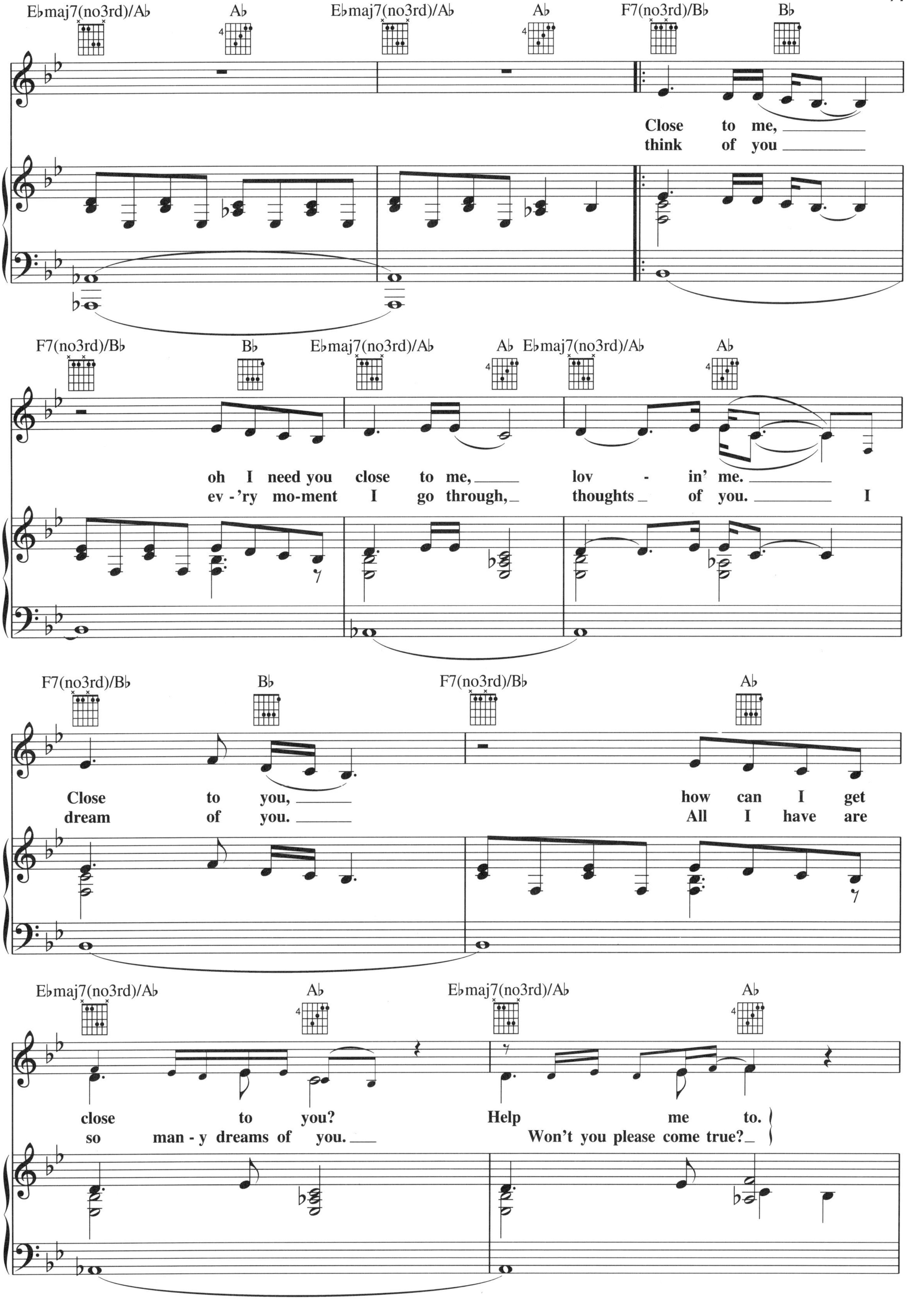
E♭maj7(no3rd)/A♭
A♭
E♭maj7(no3rd)/A♭
A♭
F7(no3rd)/B♭
B♭
Close to me,
think of you
F7(no3rd)/B♭
B♭
E♭maj7(no3rd)/A♭
A♭
E♭maj7(no3rd)/A♭
A♭
oh I need you close to me, lov - in' me.
ev - 'ry mo-ment I go through, thoughts of you. I
F7(no3rd)/B♭
B♭
F7(no3rd)/B♭
A♭
Close to you, how can I get
dream of you. All I have are
E♭maj7(no3rd)/A♭
A♭
E♭maj7(no3rd)/A♭
A♭
close to you? Help me to.
so man - y dreams of you. Won't you please come true?